T0129390

My little book of Uplifting Poems

Deborah LaBelle

iUniverse, Inc.
New York   Bloomington

My little book of Uplifting Poems

iUniverse books may be ordered through booksellers or by contacting:

iUniverse
1663 Liberty Drive
Bloomington, IN 47403
www.iuniverse.com
1-800-Authors (1-800-288-4677)

Because of the dynamic nature of the Internet, any Web addresses or links contained in this book may have changed since publication and may no longer be valid. The views expressed in this work are solely those of the author and do not necessarily reflect the views of the publisher, and the publisher hereby disclaims any responsibility for them.

ISBN: 978-1-4502-1952-5 (sc)
ISBN: 978-1-4502-1953-2 (ebook)

Printed in the United States of America

iUniverse rev. date: 03/23/2010

This book of poems I would like to dedicate to some very

Special people without their love and support

I would not be where I am today. To Mom and Dad,

And my 3 sons.

Thank you.

May the Lord bless and keep you safe.

Thank you. Love always Deborah LaBelle.

"Thank you"

You brought me into this world alone.

You gave me a loving home.

You kept me fed, clean and dry,

When all I could do is cry.

You taught me how to laugh,

You taught me how to crawl,

And you taught me how to stand,

You taught me how to fall.

You taught me how to take your loving hand.

You stood by my side every step of the way,

Along life's rough highway,

You taught me how to smile and say,

It will get better someday.

And now the day has come,

When I feel like I am someone.

You gave me the courage to go it alone,

To reach for the stars,

Reaching past Mercury and Mars.

But I would never have made it this far.

If it had not been for the love you gave me.

I would not be in this world happy,

Happy and free.

Mom & Dad.

I say to you a great big Thank you.

Table of Contents

"One Day"

One day I looked up,

And saw you standing there.

I knew in a moment,

You were the answer to my prayer.

You were my gift from above.

My gift was given with love.

I saw in your eyes a heart pure as gold.

Given to me to have and to hold.

To hold your heart right next to me,

For the entire world to see.

My gift of love that was given from above.

I knew in a moment we would never be apart.

For what we share is right from the heart.

Where you can only find true love,

You are my gift of love.

The gift of love given from above.

By Deborah LaBelle.

Why?

Why do you make her cry?

Why do you make her want to die?

Why make her heart break?

Why did you make that mistake?

Why do you make the fears?

Why do you make the tears?

Why don't you love her?

Why do you hurt her?

Why can't you answer why?

Why make a woman cry?

Why are you such a big man with a little heart?

Why weren't you that way from the start?

What has changed the man she knew?

What has changed the "I LOVE YOU"?

What is the reason for the feeling of blue?

What happened to the feeling that was true?

Now that the days have gone on by.

We now know the reason why

The reason you don't want to stay

That only the truth can lead the way

The truth of true love is the only way

To make you understand and want to stay

But this is something you do not know

And until you do you will always be on the go

So take a good look at your life to come

For it could get lonely and make you numb,

Now what you once had is now almost gone

You had made her weak but now she is strong

Now it is your time to start over again

From the beginning the beginning again

Why do you make her cry?

Why do you make her want to die?

Why make her heart break?

Why did you make that mistake?

Why do you make the fears?

Why do you make the tears?

Why don't you love her?

Why do you hurt her?

Why can't you answer why?

By Deborah LaBelle.

"Walking with Angels"

Have you ever found a friend that just touches you deep inside?

You feel a special bond that you simply cannot hide.

You give them a piece of your heart,

A view of what you are,

Sometimes they live close,

Sometimes they live too far.

It really doesn't matter,

You were friends from the start;

Soon you realize their memory is a piece of your heart.

You feel like they're an angel,

Placed here just for you,

you are always amazed at the sweet things that they do.

You don't have to see them or talk to them every day,

To know that God has sent them in His own special way.

How else could you explain?

This friendship and deep love?

It must be an angel,

Sent from heaven above.

How can you love someone you've never really seen?

The question you may ask,

Is this just a dream?

Soon you realize,

Your feelings are quite sincere.

Your friendship will continue year after year.

Funny when you talk you both seem to disagree,

I think you're the angel and you think it is me.

When you really look at it,

You have to smile and say,

the touching of our souls has taken place again today.

Tonight as I said my prayers, I prayed for my friend,

I could hardly wait until we talked once again.

For God showed me the answer,

It was really quite simple;

a soul never sees a face,

It would not recognize a dimple.

The feeling of love one feels for another friend,

The feeling of wanting to be with each other again.

Is the inner joy, that God places there,

The love one feels on top of heaven's stairs.

So if you are lucky and you have found such a friend,

Remember it is God who lives deep within.

It is God's wishes,

To one day look to see,

Angels Hugging Angels,

Perhaps it's you and me.

By Deborah LaBelle

"Walking on Clouds"

Walking on clouds is what angels do best,

When their wings need a rest.

They are always doing their best.

To lift us to our feet,

When we feel we are beat,

With golden hearts and silvery wings,

With voices soft and low,

They move to and fro,

Lifting us to our feet,

When we feel we are beat.

Smiling down on us as we go,

With eyes that sparkle with love

And a smile ever so sweet,

With a gentle hand as soft as a breeze

They help lift us from our knees

By Deborah LaBelle

Use to be:

You are now what you use to be a man
with not much feeling and free.

You want to have someone fresh and new,
it matters not how the old one feels toward you.

To be called wife, honey, lover, sweetheart, and friend.

To be held close to you, on nights that never end.

You have been my sunshine, my life, and my lover to name a few.

I hope that happiness will find its way to you.

My life has changed, but my feeling for you
in my heart will never die.

This is the hardest thing in my life I ever had to do, so I cry.

Your life will go on my friend, but mine
has come to an everlasting end.

Now our lives are nothing but dreams of old and new.

Fading hearts and love that is not true.

My hopes and dreams of a future with you

Have fallen short with only memories of you

For you in my heart, will never fade away

Now I seek only your happiness each night and day.

I hope someday we will understand, and that our love
might return on the other hand.

And to you I say, I will wait, because my heart
will never let it go away.

For you as my husband, and I as your wife,
has been the best in all my life.

So now I let you go, with broken heart, and memories of love.

Please be happy in your journey with life.

But please do remember this person and one time your wife.

Whom who has had the best man in her life,
memories, heart and dreams.

This is from my memories of your ANGEL and your WIFE

"Thoughts of You"

This is what I do every day that we are apart.

Every night when I go to bed,

Thoughts of you run through my head,

You are in my thoughts and in my prayers,

I know we have a love that is so rare,

I dream of the day we can be together,

As I know our love will last forever.

When I start to feel sad and blue

I think of you and the warmth comes through,

Giving me that warm feeling once again,

That warm feeling in my heart is from you.

Slowly with thoughts of you,

I no longer feel the pain,

The pain of being alone,

The pain in my heart is gone,

As I think of you once again,

When I see your sweet smile,

And the sparkle in your eyes,

All the dark clouds leave my skies,

When I have thoughts of you,

I no longer feel blue,

You are the sun in my sky,

And the sparkle in my eye,

The joy in my heart,

That was there from the start,

As each day goes by I think of you,

I am right back where I started,

With warm thoughts of you,

Running through my head,

I love you.

By Deborah LaBelle

"Love so Rare"

Love so rare,

Is beyond Compare.

We give it from the heart,

Where it should be from the start.

Love is beauty, Love is bold,

Love is for everyone to hold.

Hold it close, hold it dear.

Whether far, or whether near,

Love is rare, Love is beyond compare.

I give my love to you,

And hope it keeps you from feeling blue,

If you should start to,

Just remember, true love is true,

Love is rare,

Love is beyond compare,

True love comes from the heart,

Where it must be from the start.

Love so rare,

Is beyond compare

By Deborah LaBelle.

Love Is"

Love is sweet Love is kind,

True love is rare to find.

So when you find it,

You will know,

You have a gift.

A gift that will grow.

Keep it close to your heart.

As there is where true loves starts.

True love can come from an already broken heart

Or be the first you have known,

Whichever it is it will keep growing,

True love has no beginning,

And has no end,

It will be with you through every hour,

You will feel it's wonderful power.

Take you by the hand,

And lead you in a life so grand.

True love will always help you stand,

On nights that are real dark,

You can feel the love deep in your heart.

It will light your darkest days and nights

It will make you feel you have wings for flight.

You will feel you can soar like an eagle,

Up high in the sky, gliding gracefully by.

For love is sweet love is kind.

True love is a rare find.

By Deborah LaBelle.

It Started.

It started as a Child

I looked up and you smiled

I felt safe in your arms

You have kept me from all harm

But as I grew

I felt and I knew

Something was not right

A feeling had taken flight

And emptiness I do feel

An emptiness that is so real

A feeling of, I do not belong

This feeling was getting so strong

I would wonder why

As I looked to the clouds in the sky

Why I could not find, that peace of mind

The feeling of peace, I could not find

As these days keep going on by

I still wonder, I would wonder why

It felt like ripples in a pond

That would fade. And not find that bond

It keeps growing, and getting strong

Only to find it was so wrong

That feeling, that really was not there

That feeling that they didn't care

I don't know really what to do

I needed to feel wanted this is true

I really didn't know why

I would even sit down and cry

Then one day you made it all clear

Why the feeling would never be here

You had always been there for me

And now this day you shared to me

What you told me, you said it true

That my blood is not of you

The words you did say

Were another gave you away

So this is why I need to cry

To help that emptiness slide on by

For it is true Adoption, starts you out new

And gives the emptiness a brand new view

By Deborah LaBelle

In my Heart.

The letter that you sent me I hold near and dear to my heart.

I know that what you wrote is right from your heart.

The words you expressed I to know are true.

They are words right from you.

If I was granted just one wish it would be,

It would be the wish to have you with me.'

To share a life together.

Is a wish made for each other,

Even though we are miles apart?

You are still close to me,

For you are in my heart.

You have been from the start.

So I leave my life to fate,

In hopes you are my soul mate.

But if it is not meant to be,

I will always keep you close to me.

In my heart is where you will always be.

By Deborah LaBelle.

I remember the sounds of life...

I remember the sounds of every day

The children's laughter the baby's cries

The birds and the bees up in the skis

The puppies barking and the cat's loud purr

The flocks of geese in the clouds a blur

I remember the sounds of the seasons

The spring rains in the grass

The summer storms that go by fast

The falling leaves from the trees

The winter snow and the breeze

I remember the sounds of the holidays

The people yelling Happy New Year

The children saying ya Easter is here

The sounds of fireworks on the 1st of July

The sound of sleigh bells as they go on by

I remember the sounds of love

The words I need you, I love you

The words said, our love is so true

The sound of a heart beating

The sound of night breathing

I remember these sounds

The sounds of life and love

These sounds from up above

The sound of Angels from heaven

The sounds of memories I have been given

I remember these sounds

The sounds I have been given

Are in my memories and I keep on living

They are in my heart they are in my soul

I hear these sounds no more for eyes now play the role

I remember the sounds

As if I could still hear

For they are in my mind loud and clear

They are in my sight so I now see

Each sound that was given to me

I remember these sounds

For now I am deaf but life keeps on giving

These sounds I see as I go on living

Now that I have senses that will go

Please look at me so I will know

So now I remember these sounds I see

Your voice is now a memory

But please, please look at me

For life is cruel

And this is the way it is to be

By Deborah LaBelle.

"He Overlooked an Orchid"

He over looked an orchid while searching for a rose.

Little did he know that the orchid was you,

Even though a rose has its beauty it fades with time,

But the orchid stays true.

Time has a way of letting us see,

What is right there in front of us,

Sometimes it is too late,

But for you the orchid will always stay true.

So look to your mate and you to will see,

Right there beside you is the one that is true,

The one is your orchid your mate,

The one to stay true,

Don't over look the orchid,

While searching for a rose,

A rose fades with time,

The orchid stays true.

By Deborah LaBelle

Guardian Angel

I am silent with a watchful eye

I look down on you from the sky

I reach out and give you a hand

When you have problems taking a stand

I look over you as you cry

I tell you reasons why not to lie

I lift you up when you are down

I give you a smile when there is a frown

I help heal your heart when it gets broken

For I am in your mind softly spoken

I help guide you on your way

I help guide each and every day

When it is time for you to come home

I will lead you straight and not let you roam

You will be out of pain and have peace of mind

For peace at hand you will find

When it is time you will then know

The way will be shown the way to go

I'll lead your way this is true

Your guardian is watching over you

For I am your Angel from above

Looking down on you with love

Helping to guide your way each day

For God and I will lead the way

By Deborah Labelle.

"Gossamer Wings"

See them gently floating by,

On gossamer wings they reach the skies.

Slowly drifting way up high.

Up to the heavens they go,

Where they will stop nobody knows,

As they reach the heavens high,

Nar a tear drop shall they cry,

For on gossamer wings they go by,

As they reach the pearly gates,

There is where St.Peters waits.

The gates open wide to let the,

Ones on gossamer wings float by.

They are the angels that come to help you and me,

They come to help set us all free.

On gossamer wings they go drifting by.

Reaching up for the heavenly skies.

Remember when you feel down and out

And want to scream and shout.

The ones with gossamer wings

Will be there to help you out.

So watch for the ones with,

Gossamer wings as they go by.

They are the angles from up high,

With gossamer wings floating by.

By Deborah LaBelle

"Friends Abound"

Everywhere I look there are friends to be found,

They come from all around,

Some are near some are far,

But they are all around to be found,

They give us a hug and a smile so dear,

When we are feeling down and out,

Don't scream and holler and shout.

Your friends are all around,

They are the rock we lean on when we need support.

They give us the strength to get up off the ground.

With a smile and a hug that is so dear,

They are there to help lift us off the ground,

So keep smiling my dear as when you smile,

That wonderful smile that lights your eyes,

It chases the dark clouds from my skies,

You are the best friend I have had in a very long while.

Friends like you are kept close in my heart,

Where I know we will never be apart,

As when you smile that wonderful smile,

It stays with me for a very long while.

By Deborah LaBelle

"Angels all Around Us"

There are angels all around us,

If we just believe,

They are there to help when we are feeling down,

They lift us up from the ground.

We just need to believe,

There are angels all around.

When you are feeling hurt and alone,

Close your eyes and believe.

The angels will be there for you and me,

Always helping to set us free.

They walk with us everywhere we go,

Helping us reap what we sow

All we need to do is believe.

When feeling down and out,

And want to scream and shout,

The angels feel what we feel,

They help us there is no doubt,

When the tears just won't stop,

Remember the angels, all around.

They are always there to help us out,

To lift us up when in doubt,

Just remember there are angels all around.

By Deborah LaBelle

"A Pittance in Time"

A pittance in time is worth,

More than you know,

It is a moment to remember those that have gone.

Those that have gone are worth more than a pittance of time.

For a pittance in time is worth more than all that shines.

To remember those that we love so dear,

They are the ones we hold near.

They are worth more than a pittance in time.

Even without all the shine.

To remember those that have fought,

And have gone before their time.

They are worth more than a pittance in time.

By Deborah LaBelle.

"My Wish"

My wish is a simple wish for thee.

It is a wish to be happy and free,

Free from the pain I now feel,

The pain that is so real.

The pains I feel come from within.

It is a pain I learn to live with and smile.

It is a pain that is with me every mile.

But soon I will leave this world.

Then there will be no pain within.

When I leave this world I leave behind

The ones that I love that are so kind.

I know I break their hearts,

They know it is not what I wanted from the start.

I will be with them everywhere they go,

I will be the one watching from above,

I will be the one showing them love.

I will be with the Lord where no pain can grow,

There will be no sorrow, no tears to shed.

Do not weep for me, for I am in a better place.

For everyone is a winner.

Everyone is in first place.

Now that I am with the angles

They are singing with glee

For I have no more pain for you to see.

I do not wish the pain on you or me.

It was a pain that comes from within.

It was a pain that the Lord has taken from me.

I am at peace and resting here,

The lord has set me free.

Where the sun always shines,

And the birds always sing.

The flowers are in full bloom.

Like it is every spring.

My wish is that you be set fee,

Free to live most happily

I wish for you to go on without me,

And be the best you can.

For I was just a mortal man.

I know I caused you such sorrow,

And heartaches,

But for me being with you was no mistake.

You gave me great love,

That came from your heart.

And that my dear was the best part.

By Deborah LaBelle.

I can see it. Can't you?

Life as I see it can be any way you want it.

It can be as hard as you let it,

Or as easy as you want it.

You can be happy or you can be sad,

That is all up to you.

But I feel the best is to be Glad.

I can see, that is more than some can do.

I feel even that is more too.

Some can understand what they feel, others can't.

Some can understand what I feel, others can't.

I will just be Glad.

I can see the beauty the Lord has given us all to share.

From the clouds in the skies,

And the birds sailing by.

I can see the trees growing tall reaching to the skies.

I can see the rain as it hits the ground.

I can feel it too.

I can see the flowers in colours soft and bold.

From the reds to, the shiniest gold's.

I can feel the sunshine warm from the ski above.

I can see it too.

I can see the stars in the night sky, twinkling bright

And the moons silvery light,

Beauty is all around us to see.

Open your eyes and your heart.

I can see it. Can't you?

By Deborah LaBelle.

"You gave me."

You have given me hope to keep going.

You did it not even knowing.

We have never really met.

But that feeling I have keeps growing.

It keeps growing in my heart.

Where it was from the start.

It is a feeling so warm.

I know you feel it to.

For thoughts of you brighten my day.

I know in my heart it is here to stay.

Now that we have met.

After many years apart.

You will always be in my heart.

You have filled my heart with joy,

Just like a child with a new toy.

You have brightened my darkest day.

The way the sun shines it warm rays.

My nights are filled with dreams.

Dreams that you have given me.

They are dreams the world can see.

They can see the smile on my face.

You have given my heart a new home.

My heart now lives with you.

Never more will it roam.

I am no longer lost at sea

My heart is with you.

And yours is with me

By Deborah LaBelle.

Why did you say I do?"

Why did you tell the lies?

Why do you make her want to cry?

Can't you see you break her heart?

She has loved you from the start.

She promised to always love you.

But now you make her feel blue.

Now you make her cry.

And make her want to die.

You tell them she is your sister.

When are you going to wake up mister?

You are running out of life.

So why can't you say she is your wife?

Why don't you care?

She has always been there.

Why do you make her want to hide?

And feel so little inside.

She has a heart of gold.

But you are always so bold.

You tell them all the lies.

And you make her want to cry.

So late at night is when she sheds her tears.

When you are asleep without any cares.

But she knows the day is coming, she will have no fears.

She will have no fears,

And she will shed no more tears.

For you have taken from her the love

That was in her heart from the start.

So this means you never loved from the start.

You are just a mortal man that breaks her heart.

By Deborah LaBelle

"I Bend my Head"

As I bend my head in prayer.

I thank the lord I have no cares.

For I am truly blessed,

For he takes good care of me.

The lord has given me great blessings,

For each day I can feel and see.

For without his loving care, I would be drifting out at sea,

With only emptiness inside of me.

He has taken all my pains and set my heart free.

For I am one with the lord and he is one with me.

I have had some rough rows to hoe,

But with his loving hands I did them most gracefully.

For he has given me the strength,

To go it on my own.

For I know someday he will soon call me home.

And when that day comes I know where I will be.

I will be with the angles up above watching over thee,

May the Lord bless and keep you safe.

By Deborah LaBelle.

"From Above"

I am watching from above.

Sending you all my love.

Please don't weep for me.

For I am now free.

I am free from all the pain.

That took me from my love.

But you are still with me.

Even though I am above.

The angels came to me that day.

And told me it was time for me to go.

I walk with the angels now.

The angels came to call me home.

But I didn't want to leave you alone.

They told me you would not be

For I would be in your memory.

And in your heart.

Where I have been right from the start.

So I wait for you my love.

I will watch over you from above.

And sending you all my love.

I walk with the angels now,

A slow but steady pace.

For there is no race.

By Deborah LaBelle.

Calling all Angels

Calling all angels from above

All angels full of love and grace.

Help is needed for the human race,

I ask all angels for guidance and courage,

Give me the strength to keep going,

When it feels like the world is all in a rage,

I feel like a wild bird kept in a cage,

I do my best to help when I can,

Even though I feel I cannot stand.

My legs are tired and my arms are weak,

Give me the courage so that I may speak.

Speak for the mild and the meek,

I need your strength to keep going,

Lift me high so I may see,

The love that is coming to me,

From one far across the sea,

Coming to help set my heart free,

To give me a home one to call my own,

Filled with his love for my child and me,

For here on earth there is no love,

Greater than that from the Lord above,

No greater gift shall I receive,

Than the gift of love that you give me.

My heart is full to over flowing,

Like the wild flowers that keep on growing.

By Deborah LaBelle.

The World as I see it.

The world as I see it is a beautiful place to live. There are all types of creatures from large too small. How we get along is all up to each of us. I try to get along with everyone. I have a smile for everyone, even on the rainiest of days. I feel that it cost nothing to smile at someone you meet on the street even if you don't know them by name. It just may make the day go better for them. I know when someone smiles at me it makes me feel good inside. The trick is to let the smile reach your eyes. If you can do that then the smile reaches the heart and chases the blues away. I feel that a smile will make you feel that the sun is shining every day. And in a way it is for me even if it is not seen in the sky. You see I feel the warmth of the smile just like the warmth of the sun. If we watch the animals long enough they too are smiling just not the same way as you and I do, but you can see it in the eyes and the way they stand, or the way they float on the winds. They too are happy that it is a new day for them. There is so much to be thankful for in this world. We just tend to forget just what it is we should be thankful for. Well this might help some. We have all the water we need and plenty of foods to eat .We have families that care about us and that we care about. We have friends that feel the same way. We can hear the birds singing in the trees and the other animals running around while the young ones are playing. I can see young children playing in the tall grass or just sitting by a pond or lake. I can see the ducks floating on the water without a care in the world at least that is the way it seems with them. And the deer grazing in the meadows, while the eagle soars over head. A mother wolf with her young pups playing close by. I can see children laughing and singing in the parks, while the parents sit on the bench watching them. Sure there is a lot of noise as well from the cars and trucks that go by or the trains and the planes that fly over head. We have a lot of tall buildings some that people work in and some they live in. But everywhere you look there is beauty we just need to open our eyes to see it and feel it in our hearts. We has humans are slowly destroying the beautiful world we live in and how you ask well think about it the next time someone destroys a home or burns the forests. But even after a fire nature regroups to bring forth more beauty. But all the fighting that is done in the home or on the land that is what is really destroying this beautiful world we live in. If we could all just learn to get along and work together we would all be a lot better off. It would then be an even more beautiful place to live. You see when the Lord created this beautiful world he intended it to be a world of peace and harmony where everyone got along and worked together to keep it that way. Somewhere along the way we forgot about this and went our separate ways the next thing you know there was fighting among every one. And the young and the weakest are the ones that pay the price for that. We all need to learn to set our differences aside and work together to make this world a much better place to live for everyone. The way the Lord intended it to be. I pray for the day this world will see peace and harmony among every one. No matter the color of the skin, or the language spoken because to me a smile and a song are understood in any language. So with a smile on my face and peace in my heart I wish everyone the same every day that the Lord sees fit to bless you in every way.

Deborah LaBelle.

Endless Love

As I think of the true love I lost!

As cancer was the cost...

And how he prayed for me,

To be strong and yet to move on,

To find another so I won't be alone...

As time moves on through the years,

When out of the clear blue skies,

I'm truly taken by surprise,

As I find you by my side!!

My loneliness took its toll

And with you I've found my new soul

I've got so much to give

Now that your near,

I want to hold you so dear

To have loved and lost,

Was worth all the cost

Although it was sad,

For now I'm truly glad!!

I'll remember you well!!

As he spoke the words

Don't be lonely,

You have so much to give

I shouldn't be your one and only...

Please honour me with your happiness

To share your love,

To let the dove's fly above

As you find another,

So I can look down from heaven above,

And see your happiness is truly blessed,

To see your smiling face,

Filled with so much grace...

For the best prize of it all,

I had the chance to know,

The strength of your love with me,

So now I set you free

And I know you'll always remember me

And that I had the greatest gift of all

While I was on this earth,

That you were mine to love and hold!!

And that while I was there

I was your heart and soul.

By Deborah LaBelle

Mountain Air

In the pristine Mountain Air,,

With the stars so bright,

I gaze upon my one Delight,

The one and only man in My Life,

My one Desire to have and hold,

For an Eternity to be told,

As we rest on a blanket happy to have met,

In each Other's arms we feel the Charm,

The pine scented air, and the rippling water,

Here we are without a Care,

Away from the hustle and bustle,

In the Midnight air do we dare?

To hold each other tight,

As we try to conceive our

First child tonight...

By Deborah Labelle

Oh the Pain.

Oh how I feel the pain

The pain you have caused.

The ache in my heart is so real.

It is a pain I never want you to feel.

A pain that is so real.

You caused this pain

And my heart will never heal.

My heart will never be the same.

It aches for you and the loss

The loss of what was true

That loss is my trust in you.

I keep going day after day

With a smile on my face

So you will never see

The pain in my heart

Is what sets us apart,

I pray the day will come

When I will be set free

Free from the pain in me.

To feel the love I once had.

Come back to me.

Even though I feel the pain,

You are still in my heart

Where you have been from the start.

By Deborah LaBelle.

Together at Last

Today is the day that we start our life anew.

For life will have full meaning for me and you.

When I wake and sleep with thee.

You are on my mind and in my heart.

From sun rise to sunset.

That is when my mind goes back to the day we met.

We first met on the net,

I accepted you as a friend.

But now you are in my heart to the end.

My love for you grows stronger every day.

Never more will it stray.

For my love is just for you.

My love is so true.

By Deborah LaBelle.

I was born in the small town of Emo, Ontario. In December of 1956.I was raised by my parents and with two brothers older and three sisters younger. I have worked at several different jobs over the years but I never gave up on my writing of poems and short stories. They have been my way of getting through the hard times, a way for me to lose myself in my imagination. It has given me great joy and peace. I am the mother of three wonderful boys and now the Grandmother of seven wonderful grandchildren. I hope that this little book of poems gives you as much pleasure as it did me writing them.

May the Lord bless and keep you safe.

Deborah LaBelle.